God's Little Instruction Book for Mom

A Collection of Simple, Humorous, and Inspirational Sayings to Refresh You Throughout Your Busy Day.

HONOR   Honor Books, Inc. · P.O. Box 55388 · Tulsa, OK 74155

INTRODUCTION

God's Little Instruction Book for Mom is an inspirational collection of quotes and Scriptures that will motivate you to live a meaningful, productive and happy life, while meeting and enjoying the challenge and love of being a mom.

Some books have quotes and some have Scripture, but we have combined both to provide not just man's insight, but also the wisdom of God into one of life's most challenging jobs — being a mom. This little book will give you cause to ponder on motherhood, but it also will make you laugh. Some of the quotes are well-known and some are obscure, yet each quote includes a Scripture that reveals what God's Word has to say about that topic.

You will find in the last section of the book a collection of humorous and witty quotes that will lighten your load and give you a dose of the "best medicine" — laughter!

This delightful book is basic, practical and filled with the timeless wisdom of the Bible, covering topics that mothers around the world can relate to. *God's Little Instruction Book for Mom* is a welcome break from the fast-paced frenzy of everyday living. We hope that you enjoy and treasure this book as much as we do.

6th Printing
Over 270,000 in Print

God's Little Instruction Book for Mom
ISBN 1-56292-062-2
Copyright © 1994 by Honor Books, Inc.
P.O. Box 55388
Tulsa, Oklahoma 74155

Mothers are like fine
collectibles – as the years go
by they increase in value.

. . . despise not thy mother when she is old.
Proverbs 23:22

Train your child in the way in which you know you should have gone yourself.

C.H. Spurgeon

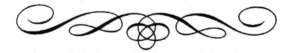

I will instruct thee and teach thee in the way which thou shalt go:
I will guide thee with mine eye.

Psalm 32:8

As a mother, my job is to take care of the possible and trust God with the impossible.
Ruth Bell Graham

And they that know thy name will put their trust in thee: for thou, Lord, hast not forsaken them that seek thee.
Psalm 9:10

When Mother Theresa received her Nobel Prize, she was asked, "What can we do to promote world peace?" She replied, "Go home and love your family."

Let love and faithfulness never leave you; bind them around your neck, write them on the tablet of your heart.
Proverbs 3:3 NIV

You built no great cathedrals
That centuries applaud,
But with a grace exquisite
Your life cathedraled God.

Thomas Fessenden

...for ye are the temple of the living God; as God hath said,
I will dwell in them, and walk in them....
2 Corinthians 6:16

Where parents do too much for their children, the children will not do much for themselves.

Elbert Hubbard

The soul of the sluggard desireth, and hath nothing: but the soul of the diligent shall be made fat.

Proverbs 13:4

If we as parents are too busy
to listen to our children,
how then can they understand
a God who hears?

V. Gilbert Beers

Let the wise listen....
Proverbs 1:5 NIV

Never, never be too proud to say, "I'm sorry", to your child when you've made a mistake.

Confess your faults one to another, and pray one for another. . . .
James 5:16

There's a time when you have to explain to your children why they're born, and it's a marvelous thing if you know the reason.

Hazel Scot

Before I (God) formed thee in the belly I knew thee; and before thou camest forth out of the womb I sanctified thee, and I ordained thee....
Jeremiah 1:5

If a child lives with approval, he learns to live with himself.

Dorothy Law Nolte

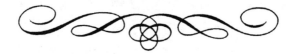

Wherefore, accept one another just as Christ also accepted us to the glory of God.
Romans 15:7 NAS

The highest pinnacle of the spiritual life is not joy in unbroken sunshine but absolute and undoubting trust in the love of God.

A.W. Thorold

For whatsoever is born of God overcometh the world: and this is the victory that overcometh the world, even our faith.

1 John 5:4

A mother has, perhaps, the hardest earthly lot; and yet no mother worthy of the name ever gave herself thoroughly for her child who did not feel that, after all, she reaped what she had sown.

Henry Ward Beecher

And let us not be weary in well doing: for in due season we shall reap, if we faint not.
Galatians 6:9

Simply having children does not make mothers.

John A. Shedd

...teach the young women to be sober...to love their children.
Titus 2:4

A mother once asked a clergyman when she should begin the education of her child,... "Madam," was the reply,..."From the very first smile that gleams over an infant's cheek, your opportunity begins."

Whately

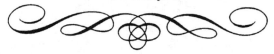

Train up a child in the way he should go, even when he is old he will not depart from it.
Proverbs 22:6 NAS

Loving a child is a circular business...the more you give, the more you get, the more you get, the more you give.

Penelope Leach

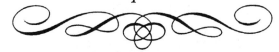

Give, and it will be given to you.... For by your standard of measure it will be measured to you in return.

Luke 6:38 NAS

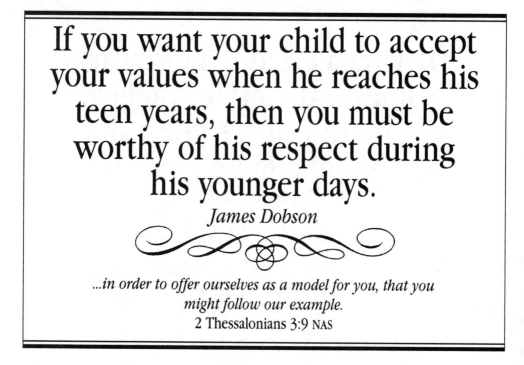

If you want your child to accept your values when he reaches his teen years, then you must be worthy of his respect during his younger days.

James Dobson

...in order to offer ourselves as a model for you, that you might follow our example.
2 Thessalonians 3:9 NAS

Women should not have children after 35 – 35 children are enough.

Unknown

Happy is the man that hath his quiver full of them....
Psalm 127:5

When we set an example of honesty our children will be honest. When we encircle them with love they will be loving. When we practice tolerance they will be tolerant. When we meet life with laughter and a twinkle in our eye they will develop a sense of humor.

Wilferd A. Peterson

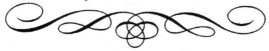

...be thou an example of the believers, in word, in conversation, in charity, in spirit, in faith, in purity.
1 Timothy 4:12

A happy childhood is one of the best gifts that parents have it in their power to bestow.
Mary Cholmondeley

Withhold not good from them to whom it is due, when it is in the power of thine hand to do it.
Proverbs 3:27

The family tree is worth
bragging about if it has
consistently produced good
timber, and not just nuts.
Glen Wheeler

A good name is rather to be chosen than great riches....
Proverbs 22:1

There is only one pretty child in the world, and every mother has it.
English Proverb

He hath made every thing beautiful in his time....
Ecclesiastes 3:11

The mother's love is like God's love; He loves us not because we are loveable, but because it is His nature to love, and because we are His children.

Earl Riney

Herein is love, not that we loved God, but that he loved us, and sent his Son to be the propitiation for our sins. Beloved, if God so loved us, we ought also to love one another.
1 John 4:10,11

Children spell "love" ... T-I-M-E.
Dr. Anthony P. Witham

*Don't be fools; be wise: make the most of every opportunity
you have for doing good.*
Ephesians 5:16 TLB

In practicing the art of parenthood an ounce of example is worth a ton of preachment.

Wilferd A. Peterson

Let your light so shine before men, that they may see your good works, and glorify your Father which is in heaven.

Matthew 5:16

Children are God's apostles, day
by day sent forth to preach of
love and hope and peace.
Lowell

Behold, children are a gift of the Lord.
Psalm 127:3a NAS

If it is desirable that children be kind, appreciative, and pleasant, those qualities should be taught – not hoped for.

James Dobson

For the commandment is a lamp; and the law is light; and reproofs of instruction are the way of life.
Proverbs 6:23

A child is fed with milk and praise.
Mary Lamb

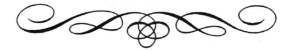

*Let no corrupt communication proceed out of your mouth,
but that which is good to the use of edifying, that it may
minister grace unto the hearers.*
Ephesians 4:29

A mother is neither cocky, nor proud, because she knows the school principal may call at any minute to report that her child has just driven a motorcycle through the gymnasium.

Mary Kay Blakely

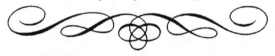

Boast not thyself of tomorrow; for thou knowest not what a day may bring forth.
Proverbs 27:1

Home is the place where the great are small and the small are great.

Glen Wheeler

But many that are first shall be last; and the last shall be first.
Matthew 19:30

You are never so high as when you are on your knees.
Jean Hodges

Humble yourselves in the sight of the Lord, and he shall lift you up.
James 4:10

When home is ruled according to God's Word, angels might be asked to stay with us, and they would not find themselves out of their element.

Charles H. Spurgeon

I will meditate in thy precepts, and have respect unto thy ways. I will delight myself in thy statutes: I will not forget thy word.
Psalm 119:15,16

The best things you can give
children, next to good habits,
are good memories.
Sydney J. Harris

The memory of the just is blessed....
Proverbs 10:7

Through the ages no nation
has had a better friend than
the mother who taught her
child to pray.
Glen Wheeler

*Devote yourselves to prayer, keeping alert in it with an attitude of
thanksgiving.*
Colossians 4:2 NAS

Give your troubles to God; He will be up all night anyway.
Unknown

He will not allow your foot to slip; He who keeps you will not slumber.
Psalm 121:3 NAS

We should seize every
opportunity to give
encouragement.
Encouragement is oxygen
to the soul.
George M. Adams

*A man hath joy by the answer of his mouth:
and a word spoken in due season, how good it is!*
Proverbs 15:23

You know children are growing
up when they start asking
questions that have answers.
John J. Plomb

*When I was a child, I spake as a child, I understood as a child, I thought
as a child: but when I became a man, I put away childish things.*
1 Corinthians 13:11

If you want a baby, have a new one. Don't baby the old one.

Jessamyn West

Chasten thy son while there is hope, and let not thy soul spare for his crying.
Proverbs 19:18

Never despair of a child. The one you weep the most for at the mercy-seat may fill your heart with the sweetest joys.

T.L. Cuyler

He that goeth forth and weepeth bearing precious seed, shall doubtless come again with rejoicing. . . .

Psalm 126:6

All that I am or hope to be, I owe to my mother.
Abraham Lincoln

Get all the advice you can and be wise the rest of your life.
Proverbs 19:20 TLB

The best academy,
a mother's knee.
James Russell Lowell

Discipline your son, and he will give you peace;
he will bring delight to your soul.
Proverbs 29:17 NIV

Mother means selfless devotion, limitless sacrifice, and love that passes understanding.

Unknown

Greater love hath no man than this,
that a man lay down his life for his friends.
John 15:13

You may give without loving, but you cannot love without giving.

Glen Wheeler

*For God so loved the world, that he **gave** his only begotten Son, that whosoever believeth in him should not perish, but have everlasting life.*
John 3:16

A mother is a person who sees that there are only four pieces of pie for five persons and promptly remarks that she's never cared for pie.

Unknown

...It is more blessed to give than to receive.
Acts 20:35

What is a home without a Bible?
'Tis a home where daily bread
for the body is provided, but
the soul is never fed.

Charles Meigs

My son, attend to my words; incline thine ear unto my sayings. Let them not depart from thine eyes; keep them in the midst of thine heart. For they are life unto those that find them, and health to all their flesh.
Proverbs 4:20-22

A torn jacket is soon mended; but hard words bruise the heart of a child.

Henry Wadsworth Longfellow

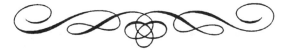

...in accordance with the authority which the Lord gave me, for building up and not for tearing down.
2 Corinthians 13:10 NAS

A mother is not a person to lean on, but a person to make leaning unnecessary.

Dorothy Canfield Fisher

There shall a man leave his father and his mother, and shall cleave unto his wife: and they shall be one flesh.
Genesis 2:24

Of all the rights of women, the greatest is to be a mother.
Lin Yutang

*Her children arise up, and call her blessed;
her husband also, and he praiseth her.*
Proverbs 31:28

Children miss nothing in sizing up their parents. If you are only half convinced of your beliefs, they will quickly discern that fact.

James Dobson

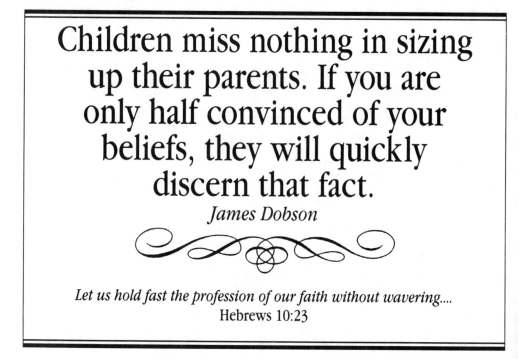

Let us hold fast the profession of our faith without wavering....
Hebrews 10:23

An infallible way to make
your child miserable is to
satisfy all his demands.
Henry Home

The rod and reproof give wisdom: but a child left
to himself bringeth his mother to shame.
Proverbs 29:15

Dear Mother – You know that nothing can ever change what we have always been and will always be to each other.

Franklin Roosevelt

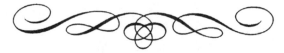

Her children stand and bless her. . . .
Proverbs 31:28

Babies are such a nice way to start people.
Don Herold

...and she conceived...and said, I have gotten a man from the Lord.
Genesis 4:1

When I come to the end of my rope, God is there to take over.

...for he hath said, I will never leave thee, nor forsake thee.
Hebrews 13:5

A mother understands what a child does not say.

Jewish Proverb

...serve him with a perfect heart and with a willing mind:
for the Lord searcheth all hearts, and understandeth
all the imaginations of the thoughts....
1 Chronicles 28:9

Children are natural mimics –
they act like their parents in
spite of every attempt to teach
them good manners.

Anonymous

Beloved, follow not that which is evil, but that which is good.
3 John 11a

The Lord can do great things
through those who don't care
who gets the credit.
Helen Pearson

*A man's pride shall bring him low: but honour
shall uphold the humble in spirit.*
Proverbs 29:23

A little boy's mother once told him that it is God who makes people good. He looked up and replied, "Yes I know it is God, but mothers help a lot."

Glen Wheeler

.... reject not nor forsake the teaching of your mother.
Proverbs 1:8

What sunshine is to flowers, smiles are to humanity. They are but trifles, to be sure but, scattered along life's pathway, the good they do is inconceivable.
Joseph Addison

A happy heart makes the face cheerful....
Proverbs 15:13 NIV

I regret often that I have spoken; never that I have been silent.

Syrus

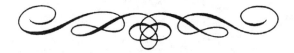

In the multitude of words there wanteth not sin: but he that refraineth his lips is wise.
Proverbs 10:19

Children are likely to live up to what you believe of them.
Lady Bird Johnson

For as he thinketh in his heart, so is he....
Proverbs 23:7

Children are the hands by which we take hold of heaven.

Henry Ward Beecher

Verily I say unto you, Whosoever shall not receive the kingdom of God as a little child shall in no wise enter therein.

Luke 18:17

The persons hardest to convince
they're at the retirement age are
children at bedtime.

Shannon Fife

Correct thy son, and he shall give thee rest; yea,
he shall give delight unto thy soul.
Proverbs 29:17

Many parents are finding out
that a pat on the back helps
develop character – if given
often enough, early enough,
and low enough.

Glen Wheeler

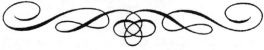

*He that spareth his rod hateth his son: but he
that loveth him chasteneth him betimes.*

Proverbs 13:24

"I can forgive, but I cannot forget," is only another way of saying, "I will not forgive." Forgiveness ought to be like a canceled note – torn in two, and burned up, so that it never can be shown against one.

Henry Ward Beecher

And be ye kind one to another, tenderhearted, forgiving one another, even as God for Christ's sake hath forgiven you.
Ephesians 4:32

Being a full time mother is one of the highest salaried jobs in my field since the payment is pure love.

Mildred B. Vermont

...for whatsoever a man soweth, that shall he also reap.
Galatians 6:7

Motherhood is a partnership with God.

Unknown

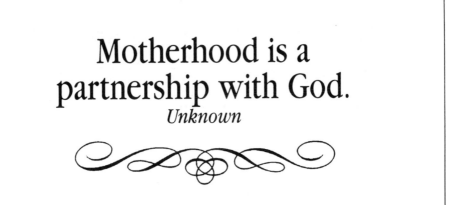

For this child I prayed; and the Lord hath given me my petition which I asked of him. Therefore also I have lent him to the Lord; as long as he liveth he shall be lent to the Lord....

1 Samuel 1:27,28

Children need love, especially when they do not deserve it.

Harold S. Hulbert

Be ye therefore merciful, as your Father also is merciful.
Luke 6:36

Too much love never spoils children. Children become spoiled when we substitute "presents" for "presence."

Dr. Anthony P. Witham

We loved you so much that we were delighted to share with you not only the gospel of God but our lives as well, because you had become so dear to us.
1 Thessalonians 2:8 NIV

A man's work is from sun
to sun, but a mother's work
is never done.

Anonymous

...her candle goeth not out by night.
Proverbs 31:18

Worry is like a rocking chair: It gives you something to do, but doesn't get you anywhere.

Anonymous

Casting the whole of your care — all your anxieties, all your worries, all your concerns, once and for all — on Him; for He cares for you affectionately, and cares about you watchfully.

1 Peter 5:7 AMP

If you have no prayer life yourself, it is rather a useless gesture to make your child say his prayers every night.

Peter Marshall

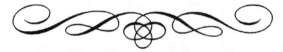

Pray without ceasing.
1 Thessalonians 5:17

The darn trouble with cleaning the house is it gets dirty the next day anyway, so skip a week if you have to. The children are the most important thing.

Barbara Bush

Lo, children are an heritage of the Lord:
and the fruit of the womb is his reward.
Psalm 127:3

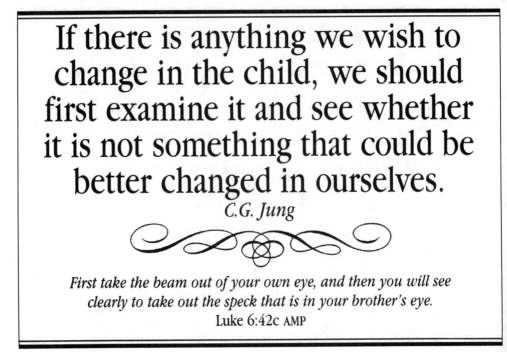

If there is anything we wish to change in the child, we should first examine it and see whether it is not something that could be better changed in ourselves.

C.G. Jung

First take the beam out of your own eye, and then you will see clearly to take out the speck that is in your brother's eye.

Luke 6:42c AMP

I remember my mother's prayers and they have always followed me. They have clung to me all my life.

Abraham Lincoln

I prayed for this child, and the Lord has granted me what I asked of him.
1 Samuel 1:27 NIV

A problem not worth praying about isn't worth worrying about.
Glen Wheeler

Be careful for nothing; but in every thing by prayer and supplication with thanksgiving let your requests be made known unto God.
Philippians 4:6

Any child will learn to worship God who lives his daily life with adults who worship Him.

Anna B. Mow

He who walks with the wise grows wise....
Proverbs 13:20 NIV

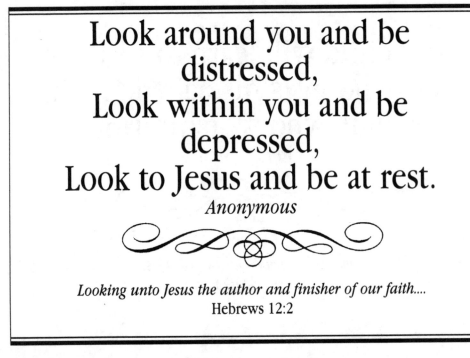

Look around you and be
distressed,
Look within you and be
depressed,
Look to Jesus and be at rest.

Anonymous

Looking unto Jesus the author and finisher of our faith....
Hebrews 12:2

A mother's love is patient and forgiving when all others are forsaking, and it never fails or falters, even though the heart is breaking.

Helen Steiner Rice

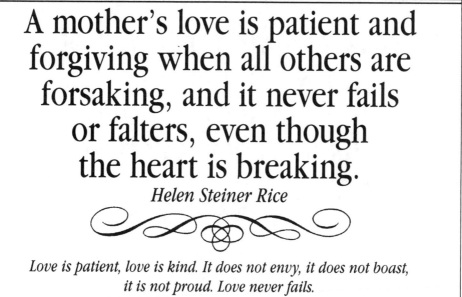

Love is patient, love is kind. It does not envy, it does not boast, it is not proud. Love never fails.
1 Corinthians 13:4,8a NIV

Making children a part of a family team is of critical importance to the kinds of adults that they will become.

Dr. William Mitchell and Dr. Charles Paul Conn

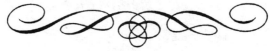

Behold, how good and how pleasant it is for brethren to dwell together in unity!
Psalm 133:1

There is no greater love than the love that holds on where there seems nothing left to hold on to.

G.W.C. Thomas

Love never fails – never fades out or becomes obsolete or comes to an end.

1 Corinthians 13:8a AMP

Every mother is like Moses.
She does not enter the
promised land. She prepares
a world she will not see.

Pope Paul VI

*Then the Lord said to him, "This is the land I promised
on oath to Abraham, Isaac and Jacob.... I have let you see it
with your eyes, but you will not cross over into it."*
Deuteronomy 34:4 NIV

God sends children for another purpose than merely to keep up the race – to enlarge our hearts, to make us unselfish, and full of kindly sympathies and affections....

Mary Howitt

My little children, let us not love in word, neither in tongue; but in deed and in truth.

1 John 3:18

Every mother has the breathtaking privilege of sharing with God in the creation of new life. She helps bring into existence a soul that will endure for all eternity.

James Keller

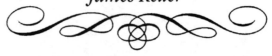

For Thou didst form my inward parts;
Thou didst weave me in my mother's womb.
Psalm 139:13 NAS

We need to be patient with our children in the same way God is patient with us.

Renee Jordan

The discretion of a man deferreth his anger;
and it is his glory to pass over a transgression.
Proverbs 19:11

A child is a gift whose worth cannot be measured except by the heart.

Theresa Ann Hunt

Behold, children are a gift of the Lord;
The fruit of the womb is a reward.
Psalm 127:3 NAS

My mother said to me, "If you become a soldier you'll be a general; if you become a monk you'll end up as the pope." Instead, I became a painter and wound up as Picasso.

Pablo Picasso

(Love) ...believeth all things, hopeth all things, endureth all things.
1 Corinthians 13:7

Our children are watching us live, and what we *are* shouts louder than anything we can say.
Wilferd A. Peterson

In everything set them an example by doing what is good.
Titus 2:7a NIV

Happy is the child . . . who sees
mother and father rising early,
or going aside regularly,
to keep times with the Lord.

Larry Christenson

*...let the heart of them rejoice that seek the Lord, Seek the Lord,
and his strength: seek his face evermore.*
Psalm 105:3,4

You can do everything else
right as a parent, but if you
don't begin with loving God,
you're going to fail.
Alvin Vander Griend

...The Lord our God is one Lord: and thou shalt love the Lord thy God
with all thine heart, and with all thy soul, and with all thy might.
Deuteronomy 6:4,5

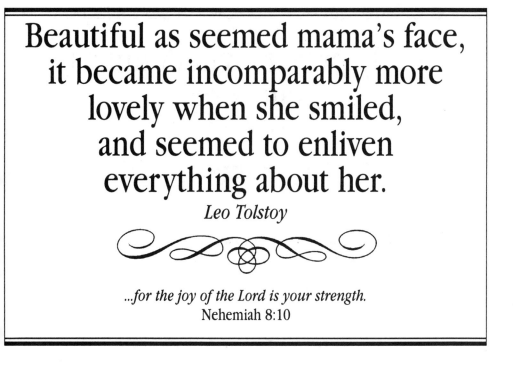

Beautiful as seemed mama's face,
it became incomparably more
lovely when she smiled,
and seemed to enliven
everything about her.

Leo Tolstoy

...for the joy of the Lord is your strength.
Nehemiah 8:10

Daily prayers will diminish your cares.

Betty Mills

Evening, and morning, and at noon, will I pray,
and cry aloud: and he shall hear my voice.
Psalm 55:17

Mercy among the virtues is
like the moon among the stars...
It is the light that hovers
above the judgement seat.

Edwin Hubbel Chapin

...mercy triumphs over judgment.
James 2:13 NAS

Nothing has a better effect upon children than praise.

Sir P. Sidney

Anxiety in the heart of a man weighs it down,
But a good word makes it glad.
Proverbs 12:25 NAS

A house without love may be
a castle, or a palace, but it is
not a home; love is the life
of a true home.

John Lubbock

Better a dry crust with peace and quiet
than a house full of feasting, with strife.
Proverbs 17:1 NIV

Many a man has kept straight because his mother bent her knees.

Glen Wheeler

. . . . The earnest prayer of a righteous man
has great power and wonderful results.
James 5:16 TLB

The more a child becomes
aware of a mother's willingness
to listen, the more a mother
will begin to hear.

A wise man will hear, and will increase learning;
and a man of understanding shall attain unto wise counsels.
Proverbs 1:5

I remember leaving the hospital...thinking, "Wait, are they going to let me just walk off with him? I don't know beans about babies!"

Anne Tyler

If any of you lack wisdom, let him ask of God, that giveth to all men liberally, and upbraideth not; and it shall be given him.
James 1:5

A sweater is a garment
worn by a child when
his mother feels chilly.
Barbara Johnson

*She has no fear of winter for her household,
for she has made warm clothes for all of them.*
Proverbs 31:21 TLB

Fingerprinting children is a good idea. It will settle the question as to who used the guest towel in the bathroom.

Unknown

But test everything that is said to be sure it is true, and if it is, then accept it.
1 Thessalonians 5:21 TLB

Any mother could perform the jobs of several air-traffic controllers with ease.

Lisa Alther

She looketh well to the ways of her household,
and eateth not the bread of idleness.
Proverbs 31:27

Parents must get across the idea that, "I love you always, but sometimes I do not love your behavior."

Amy Vanderbilt

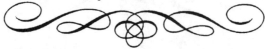

Those whom I love, I reprove and discipline;
be zealous therefore, and repent.
Revelation 3:19 NAS

Level with your child by being honest. Nobody spots a phony quicker than a child.

M. MacCracken

...in all things willing to live honestly.
Hebrews 13:18

As parents, we never stand so tall as when we stoop to help our children.

Dr. Anthony P. Witham

Be humble, thinking of others as better than yourself. Don't just think about your own affairs, but be interested in others, too, and in what they are doing. Your attitude should be the kind that was shown us by Jesus Christ.

Philippians 2:3b-5 TLB

A good laugh is sunshine in a house.

Thackeray

The light in the eyes (of him whose heart is joyful)
rejoices the hearts of others....
Proverbs 15:30 AMP

Each loving act says loud and clear, "I love you. God loves you. I care. God cares."
Joyce Heinrich and Annette LaPlaca

*Beloved, let us love one another: for love is of God;
and every one that loveth is born of God. . . for God is love.*
1 John 4:7,8

Children have more need of models than of critics.

Joseph Joubert

. . . Be their ideal; let them follow the way you teach and live; be a pattern for them in your love, your faith, and your clean thoughts.
1 Timothy 4:12 TLB

It is better to keep children to their duty by a sense of honor and by kindness than by fear.

Terence

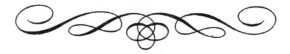

...do not irritate and provoke your children to anger – do not exasperate them to resentment – but rear them (tenderly) in the training and discipline and the counsel and admonition of the Lord.
Ephesians 6:4 AMP

(Encouragement) is the art of "turning your children on," helping them to do for themselves, not doing for them.

Dr. William Mitchell and Dr. Charles Paul Conn

And thou shalt teach them ordinances and laws, and shalt show them the way wherein they must walk, and the work that they must do.
Exodus 18:20

Home, sweet home – where each lives for the other, and all live for God.

T.J. Bach

For none of us lives to himself alone and none of us dies to himself alone. If we live, we live to the Lord; and if we die, we die to the Lord. So, whether we live or die, we belong to the Lord.

Romans 14:7,8 NIV

Children have never been very good at listening to their elders, but they have never failed to imitate them.

James Baldwin

...as ye know what manner of men we were among you for your sake. And ye became followers of us....
1 Thessalonians 1:5,6

A baby is God's opinion that the world should go on.
Carl Sandburg

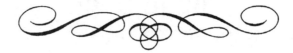

And God blessed them, and God said unto them, Be fruitful, and multiply, and replenish the earth, and subdue it....
Genesis 1:28

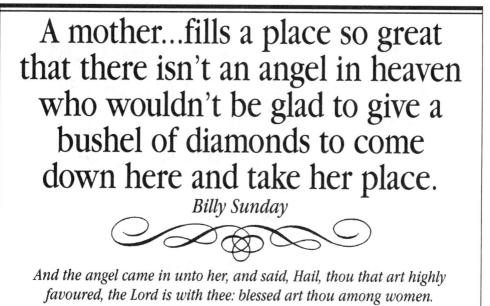

A mother...fills a place so great that there isn't an angel in heaven who wouldn't be glad to give a bushel of diamonds to come down here and take her place.

Billy Sunday

And the angel came in unto her, and said, Hail, thou that art highly favoured, the Lord is with thee: blessed art thou among women.

Luke 1:28

I have held many things in my hands and lost them all; but the things I have placed in God's hands, those I always possess.

Earline Steelburg

...for I know whom I have believed, and am persuaded that he is able to keep that which I have committed unto him against that day.
2 Timothy 1:12

A mother is the one who is still there when everyone else has deserted you.

Anonymous

If you love someone you will be loyal to him no matter what the cost.
1 Corinthians 13:7 TLB

A good deed is never lost;
he who sows courtesy reaps
friendship, and he who plants
kindness gathers love.

St. Basil

. . .for whatsoever a man soweth, that shall he also reap. And let us not be weary in well doing: for in due season we shall reap, if we faint not.

Galatians 6:7,9

Every word and deed of a parent is a fiber woven into the character of a child that ultimately determines how that child fits into the fabric of society.

David Wilkerson

You will be judged on whether or not you are doing what Christ wants you to. So watch what you do and what you think.

James 2:12 TLB

When people ask me what I do, I always say I am a mother first.
Jacqueline Jackson

Many women do noble things, but you surpass them all.
Proverbs 31:29 NIV

I think that saving a little child
And bringing him to his own,
Is a derned sight better business
Than loafing around the throne.

John Hay

*The fruit of the righteous is a tree of life;
and he that winneth souls is wise.*
Proverbs 11:30

A mother's patience is like a tube of toothpaste – it's never quite gone.
Unknown

Being strengthened with all power according to his glorious might so that you may have great endurance and patience.
Colossians 1:11

The school will teach children how to read,
but the environment of the home must teach
them what to read. The school can teach
them how to think, but the home must teach
them what to believe.

Charles A. Wells

*Teach a child to choose the right path,
and when he is older he will remain upon it.*
Proverbs 22:6 TLB

Think of the sacrifice your mother had to make in order that you might live. Think of the sacrifice God had to make that you and your mother might live.

Glen Wheeler

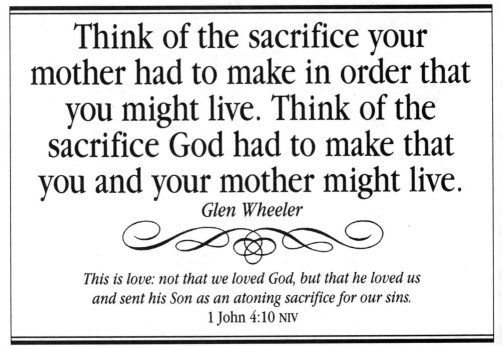

This is love: not that we loved God, but that he loved us and sent his Son as an atoning sacrifice for our sins.

1 John 4:10 NIV

Kind words can be short
and easy to speak, but their
echoes are truly endless.
Mother Teresa

*She opens her mouth in skillful and godly Wisdom, and on her tongue
is the law of kindness (giving counsel and instruction).*
Proverbs 31:26 AMP

God has given you your child,
that the sight of him, from time
to time, might remind you of His
goodness, and induce you to
praise Him with filial reverence.

Christian Scriver

*See how very much our heavenly Father loves us, for he allows
us to be called his children – think of it – and we really are!*
1 John 3:1 TLB

Your children learn more of your faith during the bad times than they do during the good times.

Beverly LaHaye

Consider it all joy, my brethren, when you encounter various trials.
James 1:2 NAS

A woman who can cope
with the terrible twos can
cope with anything.
Judity Clabes

The Lord is on my side; I will not fear: what can man do unto me?
Psalm 118:6

Parenthood is a partnership with God. . . .you are working with the Creator of the universe in shaping human character and determining destiny.

Ruth Vaughn

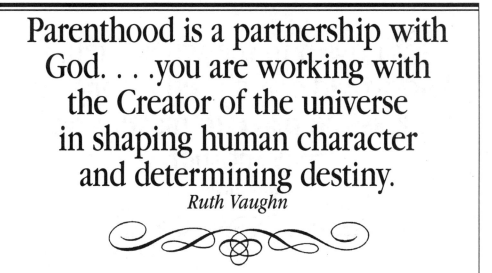

We are labourers together with God. . . .
1 Corinthians 3:9

Who ran to me when I fell,
And would some pretty story tell,
Or kiss the place to make it well?
My mother.

Ann Taylor

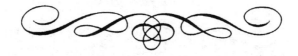

As one whom his mother comforted, so will I comfort you. . . .
Isaiah 66:13

Remember, when your child has a tantrum, don't have one of your own.
Dr. J. Kuriansky

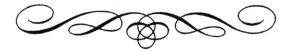

And every man that striveth for the mastery is temperate in all things.
1 Corinthians 9:25a

The only thing children wear out faster than shoes are parents and teachers.

He gives power to the tired and worn out, and strength to the weak.
Isaiah 40:29 TLB

A little boy, age eight, gave a profound definition of parenthood: "Parents are just baby-sitters for God."

Glen Wheeler

I prayed for this child, and the Lord has granted me what I asked of him. So now I give him to the Lord. For his whole life he will be given over to the Lord....
1 Samuel 1:27,28 NIV

My mother was the source
from which I derived the
guiding principles of my life.
John Wesley

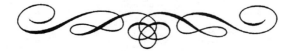

Be ye followers of me, even as I also am of Christ.
1 Corinthians 11:1

HUMOROUS QUOTES SECTION

A merry heart doeth
good like a medicine....
Proverbs 17:22

There is a right time for
everything: A time to laugh....
Ecclesiastes 3:1,4 TLB

Never lend your car to anyone to whom you have given birth.

Erma Bombeck

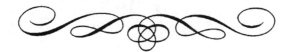

A merry heart doeth good like a medicine....
Proverbs 17:22

Parenthood: that state of being better chaperoned than you were before marriage.

Madeline Cox

There is a right time for everything: A time to laugh....
Ecclesiastes 3:1,4 TLB

The best way to keep children at home is to make home a pleasant atmosphere – and to let the air out of the tires.

Dorothy Parker

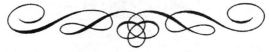

A merry heart doeth good like a medicine....
Proverbs 17:22

A mother finds out what is meant by spitting image when she tries to feed cereal to her baby.

Imogene Fey

There is a right time for everything: A time to laugh....
Ecclesiastes 3:1,4 TLB

A lot of parents pack up their troubles and send them off to summer camp.

Raymond Duncan

A merry heart doeth good like a medicine....
Proverbs 17:22

Adult education is something that will continue as long as kids have homework.

Unknown

There is a right time for everything: A time to laugh....
Ecclesiastes 3:1,4 TLB

Small boy: "If I'm noisy they give me a spanking...and if I'm quiet they take my temperature."

Coronet

A merry heart doeth good like a medicine....
Proverbs 17:22

Parents of teens and parents of babies
have something in common. They
spend a great deal of time trying to
get their kids to talk.

Paul Swets

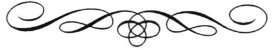

There is a right time for everything: A time to laugh....
Ecclesiastes 3:1,4 TLB

People who say they sleep like a baby usually don't have one.

Leo J. Burke

A merry heart doeth good like a medicine....
Proverbs 17:22

A perfect example of minority rule is a baby in the house.

Milwaukee Journal

There is a right time for everything: A time to laugh....
Ecclesiastes 3:1,4 TLB

If evolution really works, how come mothers have only two hands?

Ed Dussault

A merry heart doeth good like a medicine....
Proverbs 17:22

The best time to give children your advise is when they are young enough to believe you know what you are talking about.

Unknown

There is a right time for everything: A time to laugh....
Ecclesiastes 3:1,4 TLB

Ask your child what he wants for dinner only if he's buying.
Fran Lebowitz

A merry heart doeth good like a medicine....
Proverbs 17:22

Children are a great comfort in your old age – and they help you reach it faster, too.

Lionel M. Kaufman

There is a right time for everything: A time to laugh....
Ecclesiastes 3:1,4 TLB

HUMOROUS QUOTES

The quickest way for a parent to get a child's attention is to sit down and look comfortable.

Lane Olinhouse

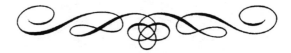

A merry heart doeth good like a medicine....
Proverbs 17:22

Children certainly brighten up a home. Did you ever see a child under 12 turn off an electric light?

Unknown

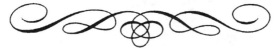

There is a right time for everything: A time to laugh....
Ecclesiastes 3:1,4 TLB

Man has his will –
but woman has her way.
Oliver Wendell Holmes

A merry heart doeth good like a medicine....
Proverbs 17:22

A food is not necessarily essential just because your child hates it.

Katherine Whitehouse

There is a right time for everything: A time to laugh....
Ecclesiastes 3:1,4 TLB

Cleaning your house while your kids are still growing is like shoveling the walk before it stops snowing.

Phyllis Diller

A merry heart doeth good like a medicine....
Proverbs 17:22

Children often hold a marriage together – by keeping their parents too busy to quarrel with each other.

The Saturday Evening Post

There is a right time for everything: A time to laugh....
Ecclesiastes 3:1,4 TLB

A baby is an angel whose wings decrease as his legs increase.

French Proverb

A merry heart doeth good like a medicine....
Proverbs 17:22

HUMOROUS QUOTES

A suburban mother's role is to deliver children obstetrically once, and by car forever after.

Peter DeVries

There is a right time for everything: A time to laugh....
Ecclesiastes 3:1,4 TLB

Any time a child can be seen but not heard, it's a shame to wake him.

Unknown

A merry heart doeth good like a medicine....
Proverbs 17:22

Insomnia: a contagious disease often transmitted from babies to parents.
Shannon Fife

There is a right time for everything: A time to laugh....
Ecclesiastes 3:1,4 TLB

Familiarity breeds contempt –
and children.

Mark Twain

A merry heart doeth good like a medicine....
Proverbs 17:22